JAMAICA BAY   AERIAL IMAGERY

JAMAICA BAY PAMPHLET LIBRARY 13

JAMAICA BAY   AERIAL IMAGERY

STRUCTURES OF COASTAL RESILIENCE

Jamaica Bay Team
Spitzer School of Architecture
The City College of New York

Catherine Seavitt Nordenson, editor
Associate Professor of Landscape Architecture

Kjirsten Alexander
Research Associate

Danae Alessi
Research Associate

Eli Sands
Research Assistant

JAMAICA BAY PAMPHLET LIBRARY
13 Jamaica Bay   Aerial Imagery

ISBN 978-1-942900-13-9

CONTACT
Catherine Seavitt Nordenson
cseavittnordenson@ccny.cuny.edu
www.structuresofcoastalresilience.org

SCR Jamaica Bay Team
The City College of New York
Spitzer School of Architecture
Program in Landscape Architecture, Room 2M24A
141 Convent Avenue New York, New York 10031

COVER
Jamaica Bay, Rockaway Inlet, view east. 1938.
source: New York City Parks Photo Archive

supported by

Cross Bay Bridge and Broad Channel, looking north, 1938
source: New York City Parks Photo Archive

Broad Channel, 1939
source: New York City Parks Photo Archive

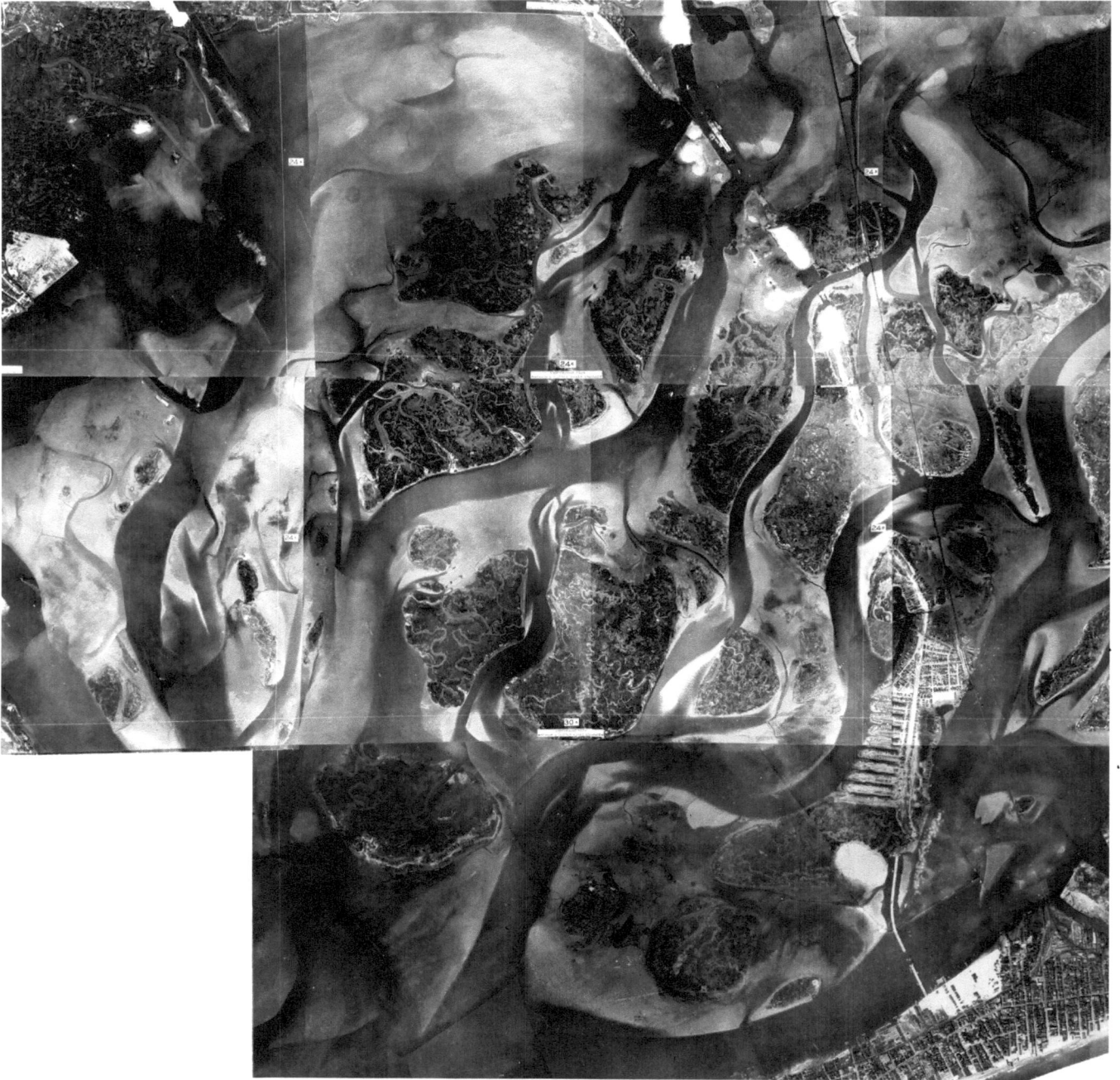

Jamaica Bay Marsh Islands and Broad Channel, 1924
source: NYCity Map - Department of Information Technology & Communications

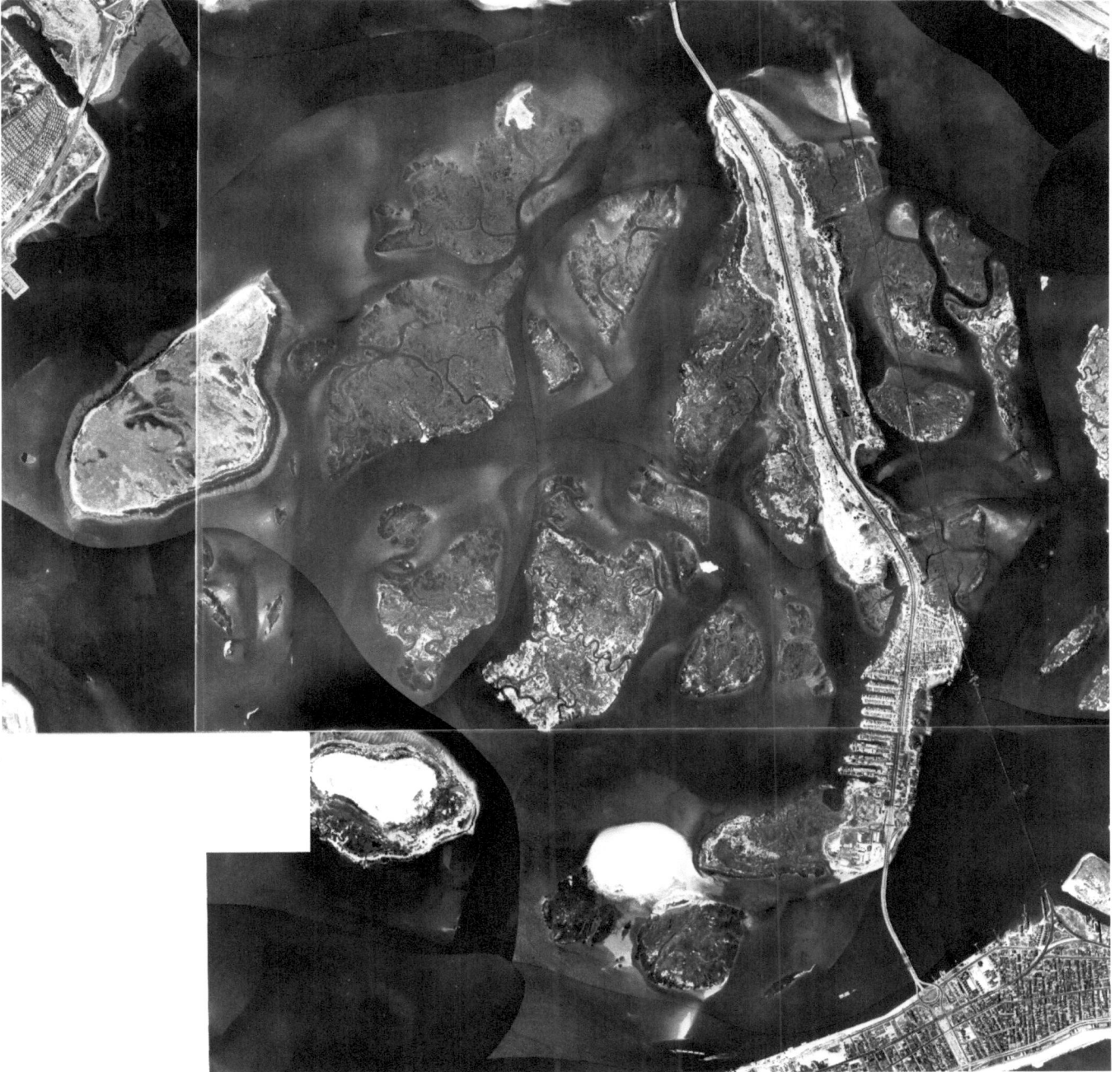

Jamaica Bay Marsh Islands and Broad Channel, 1951
source: New York State Department of Environmental Conservation

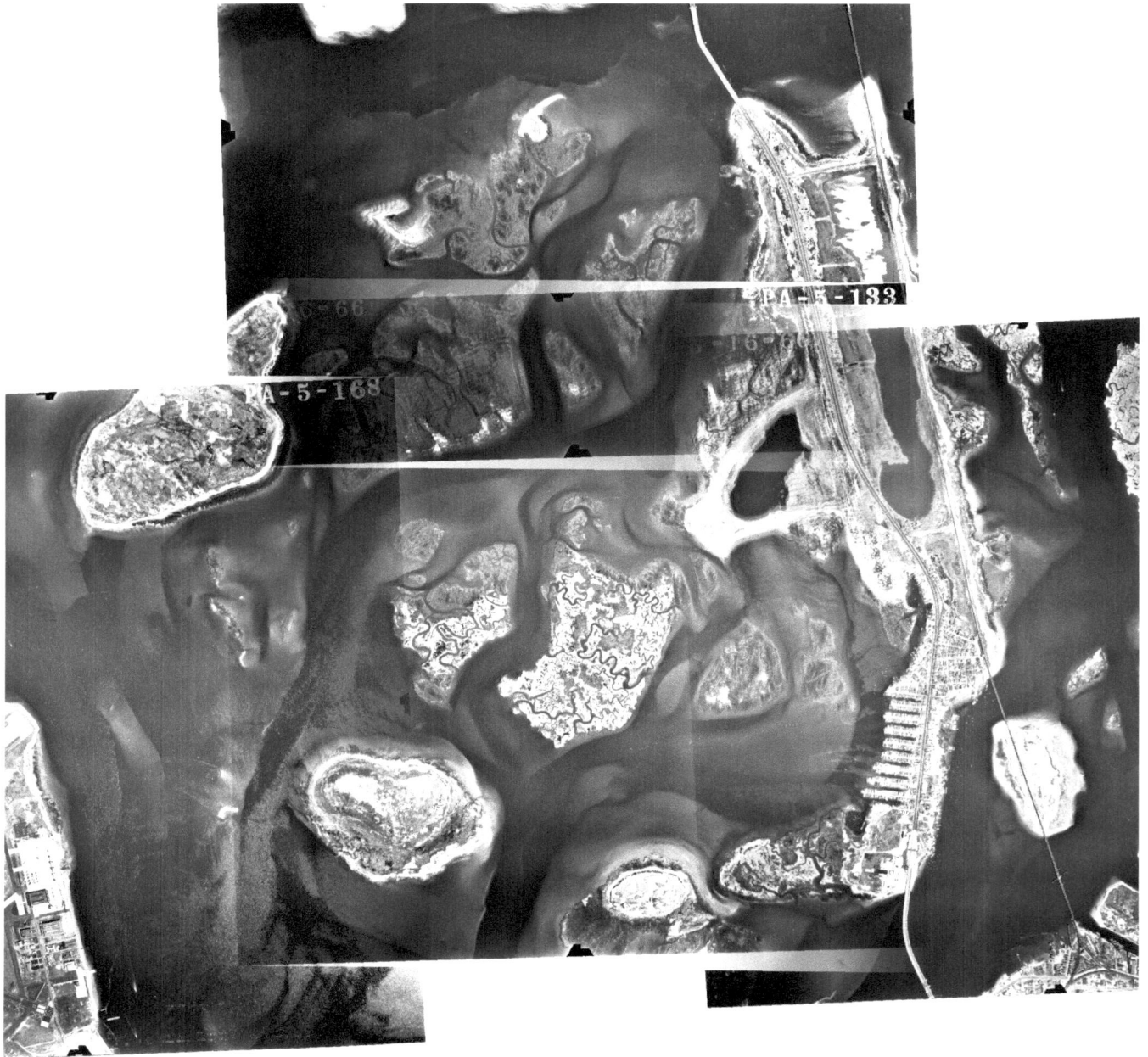

Jamaica Bay Marsh Islands and Broad Channel, 1956
source: New York State Department of Environmental Conservation

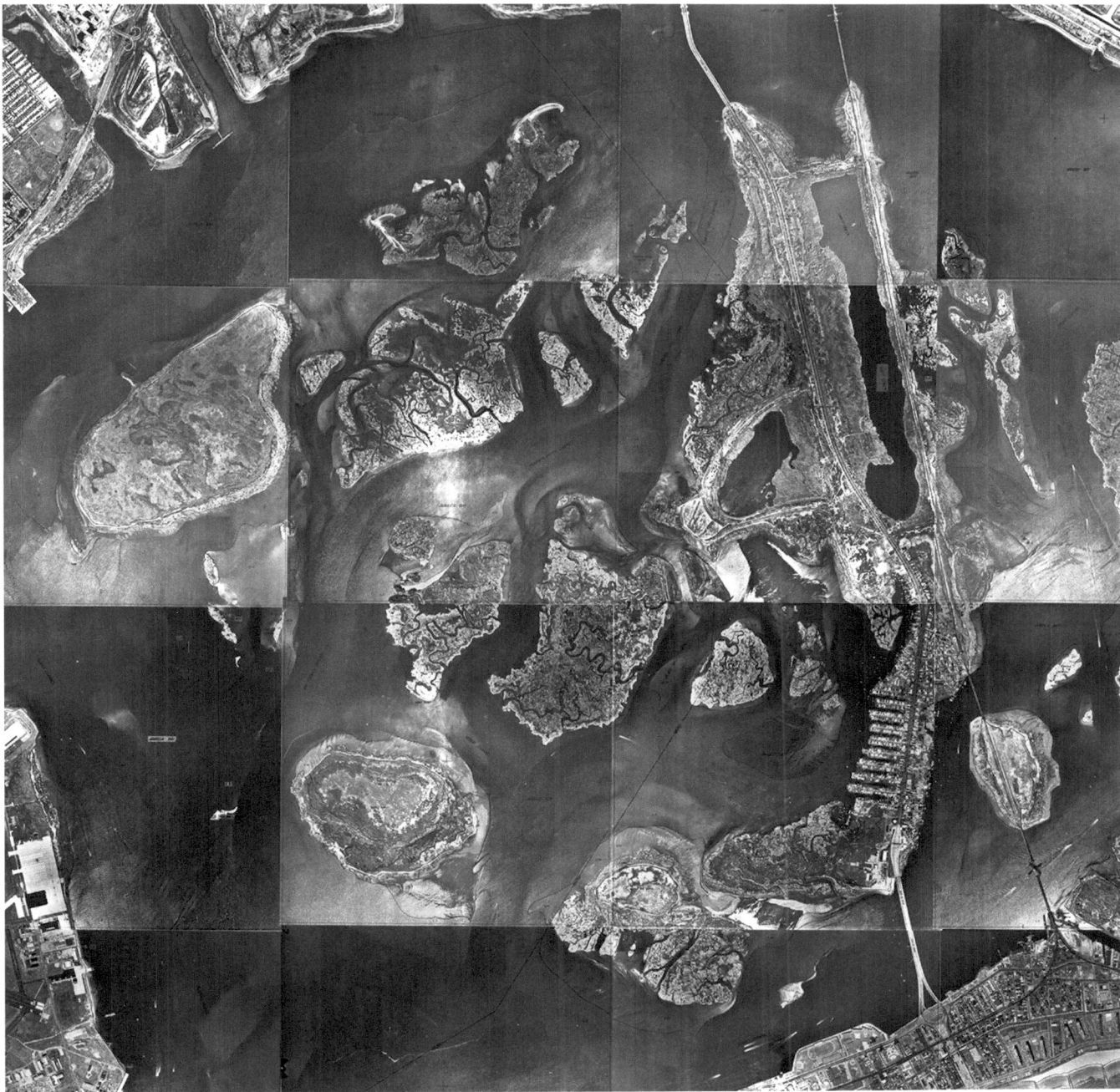

Jamaica Bay Marsh Islands and Broad Channel, 1974
source: New York State Department of Environmental Conservation

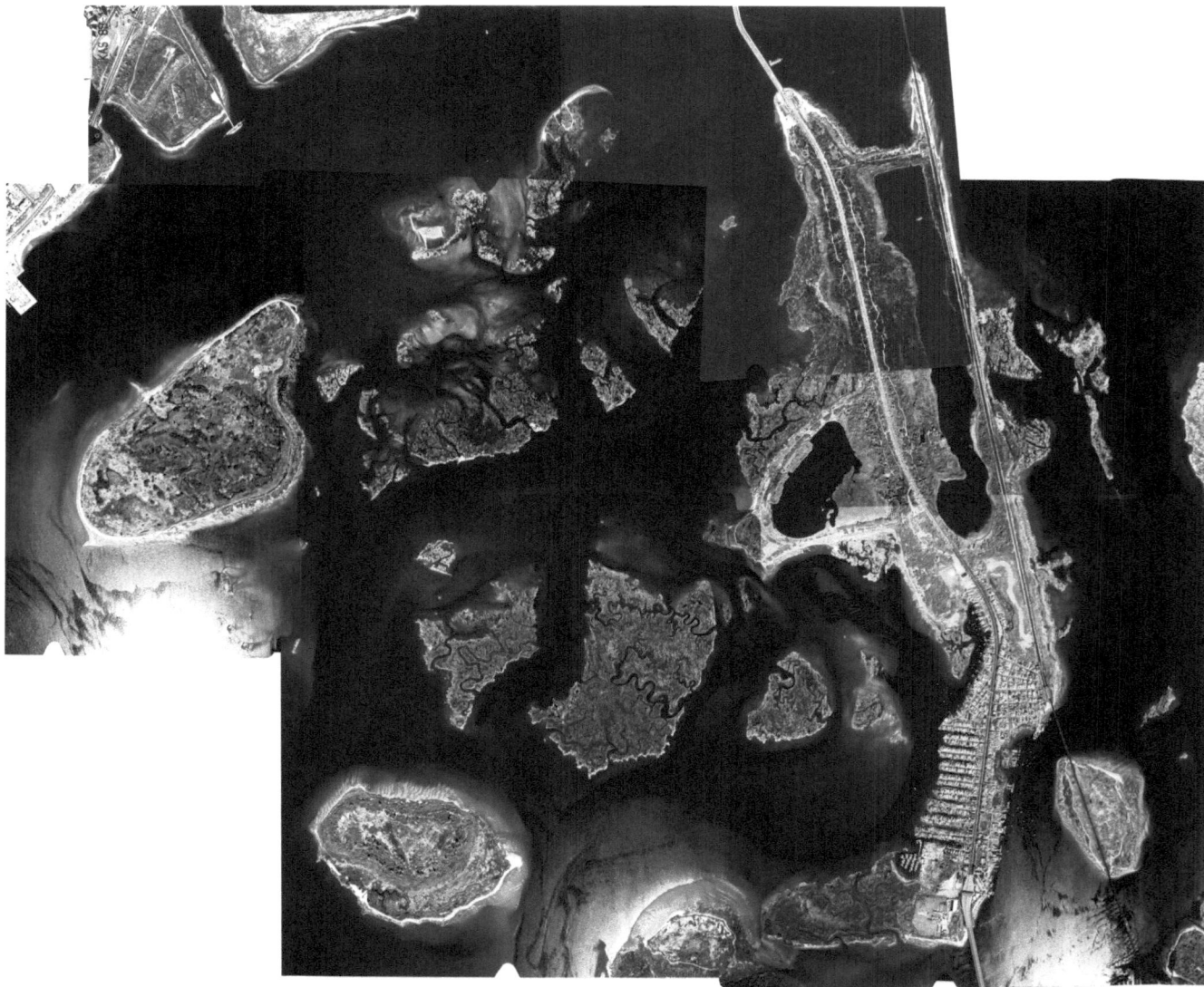

Jamaica Bay Marsh Islands and Broad Channel, 1989
source: New York State Department of Environmental Conservation

Jamaica Bay Marsh Islands and Broad Channel, 1996
source: NYCity Map - Department of Information Technology & Communications

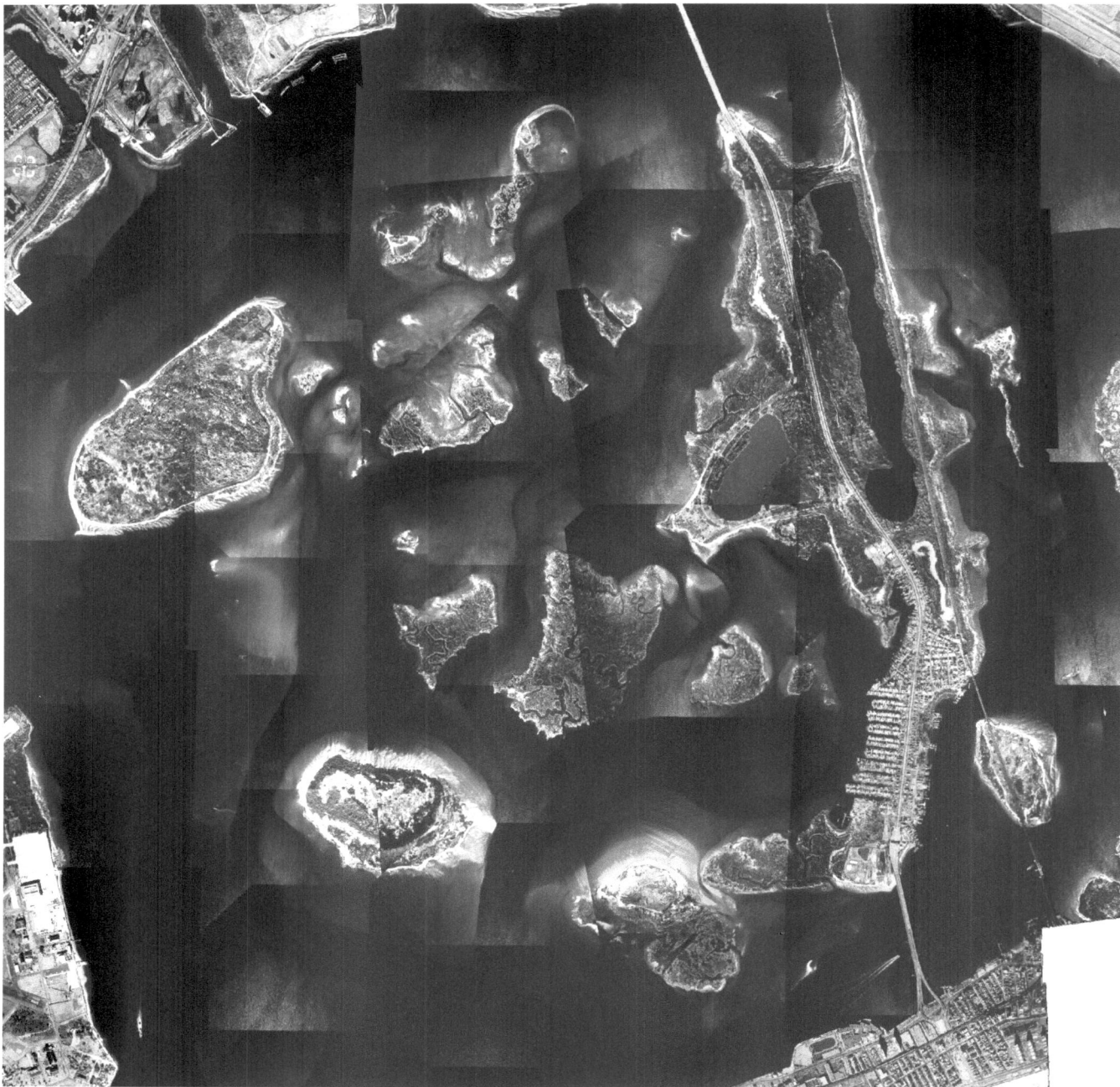

Jamaica Bay Marsh Islands and Broad Channel, 2002
source: New York State Department of Environmental Conservation

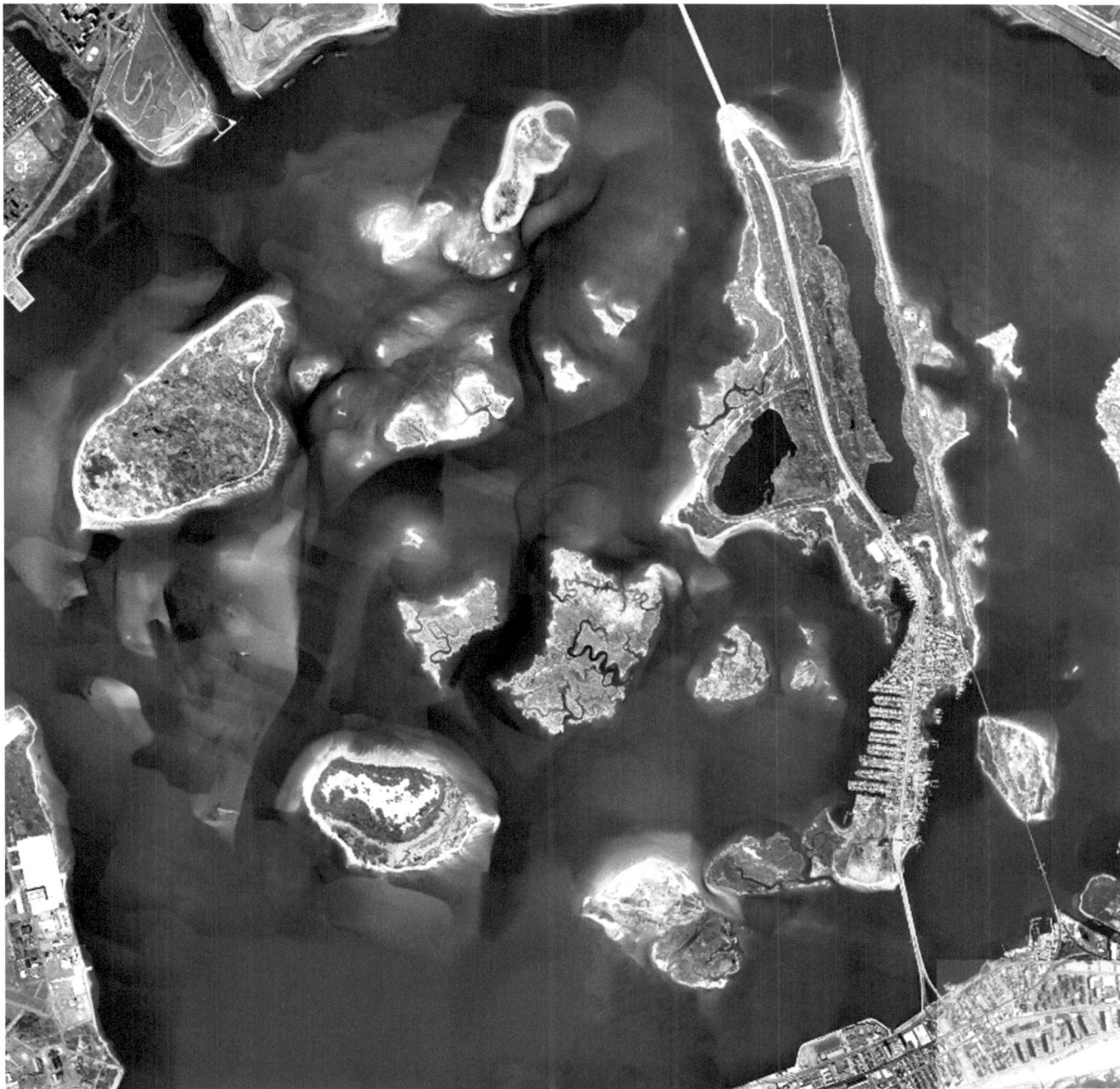

Jamaica Bay Marsh Islands and Broad Channel, 2008
source: USGS EROS

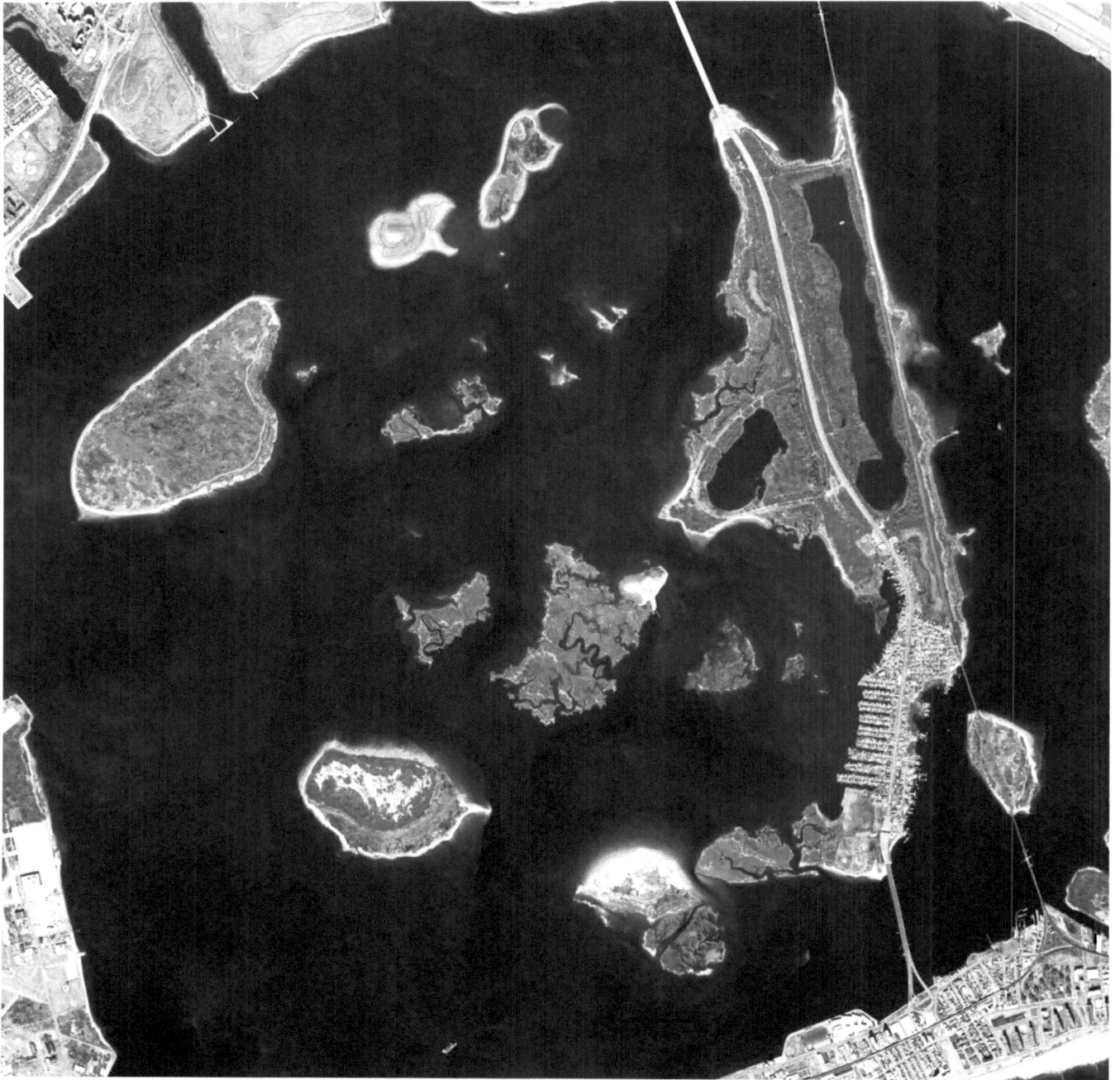

Jamaica Bay Marsh Islands and Broad Channel, 2012
source: ESRI World Imagery Map Server

Jamaica Bay Marsh Islands and Broad Channel, 2012
source: Digital Globe

Jamaica Bay Marsh Islands and Broad Channel, 2013
source: Digital Globe

West Pond

East Pond

Quadcopter camera location:
West Pond / Yellow Bar Hassock photo series

Yellow Bar Hassock

Black Wall Marsh

Rulers Bar

Broad Channel

Big Egg Marsh

Quadcopter camera location:
Big Egg Marsh / Broad Channel
photo series

Little Egg Marsh

Broad Channel and central marsh islands, 2014
source: Google Earth

Black Wall Channel, looking south, June 2014
source: © Vertigo Aerial Photography for SCR Jamaica Bay

Yellow Bar Hassock, looking south-west, June 2014
source: © Vertigo Aerial Photography for SCR Jamaica Bay

Pumpkin Patch Channel, Jamaica Bay, looking north-west, June 2014
source: © Vertigo Aerial Photography for SCR Jamaica Bay

West Pond, Jamaica Bay Wildlife Refuge, looking north, June 2014
source: © Vertigo Aerial Photography for SCR Jamaica Bay

Breach at West Pond, Jamaica Bay Wildlife Refuge, looking west, June 2014
source: © Vertigo Aerial Photography for SCR Jamaica Bay

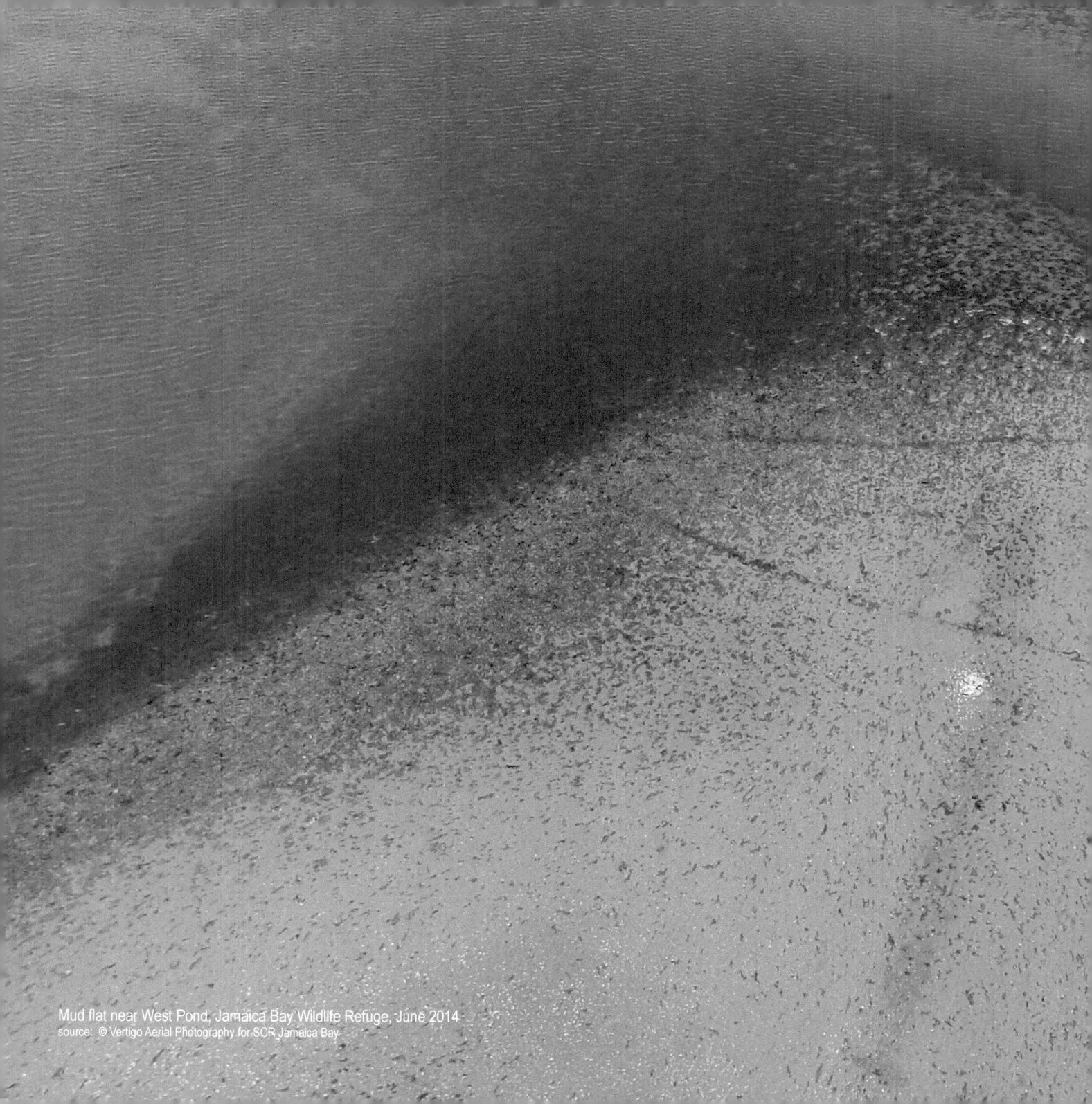

Mud flat near West Pond, Jamaica Bay Wildlife Refuge, June 2014
source: © Vertigo Aerial Photography for SCR Jamaica Bay

Little Egg Marsh, Ruffle Bar Island, and Rockaway Inlet, looking west, June 2014
source: © Vertigo Aerial Photography for SCR Jamaica Bay

Big Egg Marsh and Broad Channel, looking north-east, June 2014
source: © Vertigo Aerial Photography for SCR Jamaica Bay

www.ingramcontent.com/pod-product-compliance
Lightning Source LLC
Chambersburg PA
CBHW060827270326
41931CB00002B/85